Love For A Lifetime

Love For A Lifetime

A BRIDAL KEEPSAKE

By Karen Moore

BRISTOL PARK BOOKS

First Bristol Park Books edition
published in 2015

Bristol Park Books
252 W. 38th Street
NYC, NY 10018

Bristol Park Books is a registered trademark
of Bristol Park Books, Inc.

Library of Congress Control Number:
2014959398

ISBN: 978-0-88486-581-0

E-Book ISBN: 978-0-88486-582-7

Text and cover designed by Cindy LaBreacht

Printed in the United States of America

For Bruce,
who always treats me with love
and keeps me ever as his bride.

KAREN MOORE BARBOUR

Contents

In Honor of Your Hopes and Dreams

YOU'VE WORN a lot of hats in your life. You've been someone's precious child, lovely daughter, perhaps a sister, an aunt, or a special friend. You've been a co-worker, maybe a boss, a woman of many talents. Now you're doing something new. You're preparing to wear the new hat of a bride, and a wife... a bridal veil!

Before you reach that aisle where the music will begin to play, you'll go through a flurry of memorable activities designed to "get you to the church on time." Savor every step of the process that will take you to the altar. You will create beautiful memories to cherish for a lifetime. It is my hope that this book will serve as a reminder of all the events that make your wedding day perfect and one you and your loved one will remember from now until forever.

Congratulations on finding the love of your life. May you live in sweet joy, wedded bliss, and harmony always and in all ways.

KAREN MOORE

Dating
and
Discovery
Days

AND THEN ONE DAY YOU MET. One of the best stories you'll ever share with family and friends will be the one that answers the question, "How did you two meet?" Whether you met years ago, moved far apart, and somehow found each other again, or whether you met in the frozen food aisle at the grocery store, you have a beautiful story to share with anyone who asks.

You will always be able to warm each other's hearts by retelling that fabulous tale of your connection, perhaps on your anniversary, or with your children. There's something amazing that happens each time you simply recall everything that made it possible for you each to discover love. Catherine of Siena reflected on Divine love: *I created your soul with a capacity for loving—so much so that you cannot live without love. Indeed, love is your food.*

You have set out on a new path, and in it you will discover your great capacity for giving and receiving love. You'll learn, you'll grow, and you'll cherish all that it means to share love for a lifetime. Enjoy every step of the journey.

The Search

I made a list of all the things
I wanted in a mate,
Hoping it would help me choose,
And even help me wait.

I wanted someone special
With a heart of purest gold,
Someone who would burst with joy
Just having me to hold.

I wanted someone wise,
In all the ways that I was not,
And someone who would talk to me
About the things I like a lot.

I wanted someone who could laugh
And sparkle with the sun
And someone who on meeting me
Thought life had just begun.

I searched with all my heart
For someone I could just adore,
And then we met, and I received
This list, and so much more!

THE SINGLE DESIRE that dominated my search for delight was simply to love and to be loved.

AUGUSTINE OF HIPPO

I LIKE NOT ONLY to be loved, but also to be told I am loved.

GEORGE ELIOT

WHAT WAS YOUR FIRST IMPRESSION of the one you now plan to hold forever? Maybe you were attracted to each other at first blush, or perhaps you didn't even like each other, or simply felt no real connection. You may not have thought you had much in common or your life circumstances simply weren't right to pursue a relationship. One of you may have still been holding on to a love from the past, but then to your surprise, everything changed and your relationship grew.

Perhaps it was truly love at first sight. You knew from the first encounter that this was going to be the person with whom you'd spend the rest of your life. You even tried to convince yourself it couldn't really be true, but no matter, your intuition played on and your heart joined in. Love's arrow found you and once it touched your heart, the course of your life changed.

Your first impressions are just that, the experience of realizing there's something more you'd like to know about each other, something more you'd like to do to keep impressing each other. First impressions can make beautiful memories.

YOU NEVER GET a second chance to make a good first impression.

WILL ROGERS

FIRST LOVE is only a little foolishness and a lot of curiosity.

GEORGE BERNARD SHAW

There's Just Something About You

Something in your smile
Caught me by surprise,
And my heart was captured
By the light in your eyes...
There was just something special about you!

Something in our conversation,
Though I don't know all we said,
Simply touched my heart
And stayed inside my head,
Because there's something very special about you!

From the moment that we met,
A new song began to play,
A new melody was brought to life
That sings in my heart today.
Because there's something very special about you!

THERE IS NO SURPRISE more magical
than the surprise of being loved.
It is God's finger on your shoulder.

CHARLES MORGAN

LOVE IS NOT BLIND; that is the last thing it is.
Love is bound; and the more it is bound,
the less it is blind.

G.K.CHESTERTON

IF YOU WOULD be loved, love and be loveable.

BENJAMIN FRANKLIN

DO YOU REMEMBER your first date, that is, the official date that happened sometime after you met? As you anticipated getting together again, you may have felt a little nervous, a lot excited, and somewhat uncertain. After all, you had dated before, had tried out the whole "relationship thing" many times. Nothing magical really happened, nothing stood out to make it all seem special.

Yet, this time, there was something new in the wind. Something you couldn't quite explain to yourself had made its presence known. Something had happened that caused you to hope a little, to want to test the waters one more time, tempting fate perhaps, but giving yourself a chance to discover love again. Oh, even the thought of it was scary.

First dates are important because they begin to share the picture of possibility. They begin to help you see the gift of hope they may contain. Maybe you went to an informal restaurant for lunch that first time or perhaps you simply talked over lattes or a little wine and set the foundation for further conversation. All you know now is that whatever you did on that first date, you chose to move on to a second date, to give yourself more time to explore just what this relationship could be. First dates take a little courage, a lot of hope, and an open heart. Fortunately, you had all of those.

On Our First Date

I thought about our first date,
Long before we even met,
Knowing it would be a day
I never would forget.

I pictured how I'd smile
And fill your ears with nervous chatter,
Though nothing I would say just then
Would prove to really matter.

But something would be different,
It would be destiny or fate,
For we would know from that day on
We'd had our last first date.

GRAVITATION cannot be held responsible for people falling in love.

ALBERT EINSTEIN

YOU LEARN to love by loving.

FRANCIS DE SALES

Cupid
steadies her aim,
unleashes her arrow,
and pierces an unsuspecting heart
with love.

DATING IS A BIT like running a race,
though it often requires better shoes.

LOVE IS a springtime plant that perfumes
everything with its hope, even the ruins
to which it clings

GUSTAVE FLAUBERT

THE GREATEST HAPPINESS in life is the conviction
that we are loved—loved for ourselves, or rather,
loved in spite of ourselves.

VICTOR HUGO

Dating Again

Put aside experience,
The best is yet to be,
Let joy affirm your soul,
And set your spirit free.

Your Smile Speaks to Me

Your smile speaks to me
And I am warmed by your eyes.
I feel the touch of your hand
And I am calmer and happier,
Connected to the world in ways,
I've never known before.
I sense your joy in being near me,
And I'm aware of the gifts you bring to my life.

THERE'S A BLUSH for won't and a blush for shan't
And a blush for having done it;
There's a blush for thought and a blush for naught
And a blush for just begun it.

JOHN KEATS

DATING keeps your love-light on.

The Dating Dance

He nodded.
So did I.
We headed for the swarm of warm,
heated movement on the dance floor.
He looked absently about,
Sometimes noting he had a partner, sometimes not.
I casually observed; seeing nothing,
    seeing everything.
One swift movement and our hands touched
as he whirled me around.
The music stopped.
So did I.
One more song and we danced again,
    slower this time.
The movement continued, elbows, fingers, toes...
swirling, whirling, side to side, note by note.
Our eyes met, He smiled.
So did I.
The dance continued.

WHEN YOU STARTED this relationship, you might not have been thinking it would turn into love. You may have hoped or dreamed or imagined the possibility, but other dating experiences had taught you not to expect too much and certainly not to get carried away with your dreams.

But then...it happened! Before you actually grasped the reality of it, your heart was doing some kind of summersault and your eyes betrayed the joy you were feeling each time you met. You blushed at the very idea and yet, it was real; not just for you this time, but for both of you. It was mutual!

No one can truly understand why people fall in love. Sometimes the most unlikely people meet and bond and become a couple. Sometimes, couples seem absolutely made for each other. The good news is that it doesn't matter what anyone else thinks about the love you share with each other because it's all about the two of you, what you think and what the two of you want.

It all begins in the heart and only the heart knows how to tenderly embrace love.

What the Heart Knows

The heart is a dreamer,
And wanders alone,
Seeking love's call
All on its own.

It knows there is something,
Not easily defined
That will bring it true joy
And sweet peace of mind.

For the heart knows for sure
That nothing means more
Than discovering a love
Like never before.

So for all of the dreamers
And those hoping for bliss,
May your hearts fill with love
From the very first kiss.

NOTHING IS MORE TRUE, more real, than the
primeval magnetic disturbances that two souls
may communicate to one another, through the
tiny sparks of a moment's glance.

VICTOR HUGO

YOU MAY NOT HAVE BEEN conscious of actually making the choice to only date each other. After dating a few times, you probably just discovered that neither of you really wanted to go out with someone else. It seemed easy. Becoming exclusive meant that you could begin to act as a couple and set some guidelines for what you wanted your relationship to become. You could begin to think in terms of being "us" and "we." It was such a good feeling and it launched the relationship in a significant way.

The gift of dating is that you get to learn about each other. You identify each other's quirks and habits, and you listen to one another and experience life in new ways simply because you're together. You share your hopes and aspirations, your foibles, and your favorites. It's the beginning of a journey and it gives you a glimpse into the future.

As you look back over your relationship, this is the time period that will offer you foundational moments, ones that provided depth and significance. Recalling these moments as the years go by, will always strengthen your relationship no matter what else is going on in your lives. Tell your favorite stories to each other over and over again. They will bring you continual joy.

Just Me, Just You

There's something really wonderful,
About being me and you,
Laughing, talking, holding hands
Loving all we do.

We're growing closer by the day,
And we're connected heart to heart,
We may not know the future yet,
But we're off to a great start.

LIFE HAS TAUGHT us that love does not consist in gazing at each other but in looking outward together in the same direction.

ANTOINE DE SAINT EXUPÉRY

IT IS BY LOVING and by being loved that one can come nearest to the soul of another.

GEORGE MACDONALD

THIS IS THE MIRACLE that happens every time to those who really love; the more they give, the more they possess.

RAINER MARIA RILKE

LOVE IS A SMOKE made with the fume of sighs.

WILLIAM SHAKESPEARE

AND THEN it became time to meet the families. You may vividly remember the first time you went to visit each other's parents. You couldn't help but wonder if they would like you and if you would all feel like family one day. You'd heard the good things about each family member and even a little of the challenges they had faced in life. It was a meeting fraught with mixed emotions and more than a little joy. After all, these were the people who provided the history, the roots and the opportunity to see the one you love in a different context. You could hear the stories of growing up, of holidays, and of escapades at school.

The beautiful thing though is the realization that you were special enough to each other that you wanted to invite your families into your relationship. You wanted to begin to share the things you had come to know and love about each other, and give your families a chance to share in your happiness.

It's safe to say that the members of the family were just as nervous about meeting you, just as anxious that things would go well. Yes, meeting the family is a milestone and one that helps pave the way to the future.

It's So Nice to Meet You

Your nerves were slightly wacky,
Your smile somewhat strained,
You practiced just what you would say
And felt a little drained.
You smiled very kindly,
As you met each one by name
And tried to hide your nervousness,
As they tried to do the same.

Once you got to talking,
Things were off to a great start
And before you even knew it
You shared stories from your heart.
How quickly then, time slipped away
And when it was all through,
They said as you all hugged good-bye,
"It was so nice to meet you!"

The Proposal

PROPOSAL STORIES abound, some with unique flare, some with bended-knee, and some with utter surprise that the words were actually spoken. Your story has its own beauty, its own unique blend of nervous joy and tenderness. You may relive the moment, the day, the place where you stood or the thoughts that filled your mind when first you heard the words that would bring you to the altar. After all, this was the moment of a lifetime and one your heart will play forever as though it happened yesterday.

Whether your fiancé dropped down on one knee and took you by surprise, or simply took your hand and shared his heart and soul, letting you know that he did not want to live without you any longer, that moment is the beginning of the rest of your life; the first of many beautiful stories you ll share as a couple. It will be a defining moment, one that changed the course of your history and gave your life a dimension it could never have enjoyed before.

A proposal of marriage is a new song, never to be taken lightly, never to be forgotten, for it begins the dance of a lifetime. Celebrate the day you heard those amazing words, the ones that filled you with joy and challenged your heart to respond with its greatest truth and love. Tell each other the story of what you felt and what you thought when those words were spoken, "Will you marry me?"

THE ONES YOU LOVE in your heart are but guests in your soul.

JIM COTTER

LOVE is a great beautifier.

LOUISA MAY ALCOTT

LOVE CURES people, both the ones who give it and the ones who receive it.

KARL MENNINGER

A LOVING HEART is the truest wisdom.

CHARLES DICKENS

THE HUNGER FOR LOVE is much more difficult to remove than the hunger for bread.

MOTHER TERESA

Join Me at the Altar

Come join me at the altar
And be my lifelong bride,
Be my sweet companion
And my confidante and guide.

I promise that I'll be your friend,
And listen with my heart
And I promise that I'll always strive
To love you more and do my part.

If you'll stay close beside me
Through all life brings our way,
Then we can face the challenges
And joys that fill each day.

Yes, join me at the altar
And I pledge to help you see
That our love was meant to last,
And you were meant for me!

I ASK YOU to pass through life at my side—to be
my second self, and best earthly companion.

CHARLOTTE BRONTË, *JANE EYRE*

MY MOST BRILLIANT achievement was my ability to be able to persuade my wife to marry me.

WINSTON CHURCHILL

WHAT GREATER THING is there for two human souls than to feel that they are joined... to strengthen each other... to be at one with each other in silent unspeakable memories.

GEORGE ELIOT

GROW OLD along with me, the best is yet to be.

ROBERT BROWNING

NO ONE ELSE will ever hold my heart the way you do.

AUTHOR UNKNOWN

LOVE IS A CANVAS furnished by nature and embroidered by imagination.

VOLTAIRE

Finding the Right Words

He may have stumbled through the words,
Or said everything just right,
But the day he popped the question
Filled your heart with sweet delight.

It wasn't easy for him
To find just the words to say
That meant you'd make a promise
To share your life and love that day.

Yes, that question popping moment
Changed your world and made it spin
Into a new direction
Where a new life could begin.

For it's more than just the words,
It's more than just a ring,
For now you have a lifetime love
Which means more than anything.

PERHAPS I'M NOT your first date, your first
kiss, or your first love, but I want to be your
last everything. With the proposal, comes the
beginning of your story, a new story of a future
made for two. It will be one of your favorite
love stories ever and you'll never grow weary

in the telling of it. What joy it will bring to your heart each time you recall that moment, those precious words, and all that you had to consider to be sure that "yes" was the answer.

You may never be a perfect couple in the eyes of others, but you'll always be a perfect couple for each other as long as you embrace the future together and create the spaces that allow you to grow and change and become all that you're meant to be together, because getting married means that you say "I do" with every sunrise.

As You Move Beyond "I Do!"

The love you share is tender,
Its promise bold and true,
But the love you feel
becomes more real
With each day ahead of you.

Bravely step into the future,
For all along the way
The love you know
will gently grow
Stronger day by day.

YOU'RE ENGAGED! Since you're holding this book, we know your answer was "yes." What we don't know is if you had an immediate "yes" or if you had to think about it. Maybe you put the answer off for a few weeks or months. Maybe you weren't ready for a full time commitment. Or maybe your "yes" had waited so long for the question to be asked, that a heart-felt response was easy for you.

Whatever it took to get to the "yes" moment, your heart is sure to capture it so that it is always camera ready. You will never forget the feeling and the delight of discovering that dreams really do come true. Suddenly the world held more promise, for you were making a decision to become a couple, to give up the single life and align your goals with those of your beloved. It was a new day, a life-changing day!

Did your proposal come complete with a ring or did you shop for an engagement ring together? If you shopped together, you were probably a bit giddy as you figured out the right style for you, whether you would wear a diamond or another gemstone, or whether you would wear a family heirloom.

Whatever you decided, the moment you slipped the ring on your finger, you knew you had made the right choice. You knew that you were ready to commit your heart to the love of your life. From this day forward, each time you look at that ring, you'll know you are loved and that you are no longer living on your own in the world. Share your thoughts often with your beloved of all that it means to wear your beautiful engagement ring. It's a story you'll want to tell over and over again.

Engagement traditions have changed over time. Our ancestors used everything from string to wire to indicate a promise had been made between two people. It was the Archduke Maximilian of Austria who is given credit for giving the first diamond engagement ring to his beloved in 1519. Though the tradition didn't truly catch on until two decades later, the die had literally been cast.

Today, colored diamonds and other gemstones are used as engagement rings, but whatever jewel is chosen, the most glowing gem of all is the love you share. Perhaps you stuck with tradition or created your own engagement ring, but whatever choice you made, your new life began that very day. The memory of receiving the ring will be a keepsake forever.

The Marriage Proposal

I'll remember that moment
For the rest of my life,
The one where you whispered
"Will you be my wife?"

You were tender and nervous,
A little unsure,
With a hope in your eyes
I never noticed before.

You took my hand
And held it so very tight
As you waited for the answer
That would make things all right.

I was awestruck and marveled
At what you had done
And the promise you offered
To make our lives one.

You may have thought I waited,
To make you have to guess,
But I choked back tears of joy,
To answer with a "yes!"

The Question

Before I give my life to you,
Or offer you my hand,
Before I let the future in
Please help me understand...

Is there a heart that you hold still
That fills you with regret,
Some past love that will remain
That you never can forget?

Is there any part of all you plan
In the future we would share,
Where you don't see me stepping in
And always being there?

Is there a need that you might have
That I cannot fulfill?
Would you to seek a former love
That you would hold to still?

Could you withdraw your love one day
And take away my claim,
Saying this was a mistake
And I was all to blame?

Yes, now's the time to tell me
If you've cause to hesitate,
For if you don't, then I am yours
And my love can hardly wait.

THERE IS NO REMEDY for love but to love more.

HENRY DAVID THOREAU

WHO WAS THE FIRST PERSON you called or spoke to after you were engaged? Did you tell strangers on the street that you were in love? Did you call you parents or your best friend? There's nothing quite as sweet as sharing the happy news that comes with getting engaged. Tears of joy fill the eyes of the people who love you both, who always hoped you'd find real happiness. Everybody wants the best for you and the next weeks and months will find you telling your love story over and over again. It's okay though. It's a great story and just hearing it encourages everyone around you.

Perhaps you sent out a formal announcement letting people far away know about the change that would be coming into your life. Perhaps you simply savored the joyful news with a few close friends. Whatever you did, once the word got out, the inevitable questions began.

When will you marry? Where will you have a ceremony? Who will be invited? It's tempting to try to answer all those questions, but the truth is, you don't have to know the answers just yet. You don't have to know anything except that you have found your soul mate, your life partner, the person who will hold you close when you need a hug or give you encouragement or a moment of tenderness. You have the one person who will come to know you better than anyone else has ever been able to do, for this is the person who will share your heart, your secrets, your hopes and your dreams. This is the person who will seek your good in all things and who will applaud your accomplishments and lift you up again when you fail. This is the person who will have the greatest impact on your life that any human being can have upon another. Yes, this is your beloved and that's the reason you share your good news with gusto. You have found the one. Nothing could be more wonderful.

Shout It to the Mountaintops

I'd shout it to the mountain tops,
I'd raise my voice up high,
Letting all my happiness
Fill the earth and sky.

I'd tell it to the blue-green grass
And to the hills and trees,
I'd tell it to the flowers
As they dance with honeybees.

I'd tell it to the neighbors
And to the kids across the street,
And I'd tell it to my friends
And anyone I might meet.

Yes, I'd tell everyone who'd listen,
My heart's as full as it can be,
Because someone "popped the question"
And wants to marry me!

WHATEVER OUR SOULS are made of,
his and mine are the same.

EMILY BRONTË

TWO SOULS, one heart.

FRENCH PROVERB

THE ARMS OF LOVE encompass you with your present, your past, your future, the arms of love gather you together.

ANTOINE DE SAINT-EXUPÉRY

WHAT A HAPPY and holy fashion it is that those who love one another should rest on the same pillow.

NATHANIEL HAWTHORNE

My heart to you is given:
Oh, do give yours to me;
We'll lock them up together,
And throw away the key.

FREDERICK SAUNDERS

WHEN BRUCE AND I became engaged we went to one of our favorite Italian restaurants and, since it was a nice evening, we walked there from my apartment. Feeling still a bit giddy about the new diamond ring on my left hand, we enjoyed sharing the news of our engagement with the woman who waited on us. She was very kind and gracious and made sure we had everything we needed to make the evening special. She even brought candles to our table and sweet pink and purple flowers to make the whole event more memorable.

I teased her that all we needed were violins, as we sipped our champagne and enjoyed the ambience. She smiled and walked away to place our order. After we enjoyed our first course and the salad we shared as our main course, she asked if we'd like some dessert. We thought some gelato would be nice. She came back to the table with her daughter who had been attending the gelato counter. They smiled and said that they wanted to sing a song to celebrate our engagement. They leaned in to us and started softly singing *At Last*. We wept. *At Last* is our love song, our theme, our sense that God has heard our prayers. Of all the songs they might have chosen, they sang OUR song. It was incredible. We felt such love and affirmation. Only God could orchestrate such delight. We will remember that special night for many years to come.

A LOVING HEART is the beginning
of all knowledge.

THOMAS CARLYLE

Wonderful
Wedding
Plans

NOW IT'S TIME to switch into high gear and begin to plan your wedding. Initially, you have to decide what time of year to get married and where you would like the ceremony to take place. Would it be an intimate affair with close friends? Or a big splash with all the trimmings and relatives you might not know? After discussing options with your family and friends you may choose a simple setting or something more formal; something elegant, or a sweet trip to city hall.

With an array of such choices, your checklist may feel overwhelming. After all, you're making one of the biggest decisions of your life and you want everything to be perfect. Perfect for you may come with a horse-drawn carriage to the big church on the square, or it may come with a new passport and an ocean cruise. Perfect can only be described by you, can only be done your way.

Beyond the type of wedding, you have to consider everything from what to wear, how to word your invitations and set your budget, readings for the ceremony, attendants, flowers and photographers, and the vows you will share. The best part of the planning is in knowing that when all is said and done and you whisper "I do!" to the love of your life, everything will be different. You will begin a new life, together.

The Wedding Plans

Should we marry in the summer,
Or the winter or the spring?
Should we plan a big reception
Or a family gathering?

Should we pick a favorite song
Or write each word to say,
Send a formal invitation
Or just announce the wedding day?

Should we be elegant or casual,
Have an awesome six-piece band,
Wear a gown and a tuxedo,
Should we kneel or sit or stand?

Should we fill the church with people
Or just a special few,
Or should we plan to wed at home
With just a friend or two?

Yes, there's so much to consider,
So much to plan with great delight,
Because you chose your lifetime love
And the future's warm and bright.

PLANNING is bringing the future into the present so you can do something about it now.

ALAN LAKEIN

IN DREAMS and in love there are no impossibilities.

JAMES ARANY

TO ACCOMPLISH great things, we must not only act, but also dream; not only plan, but also believe.

ANATOLE FRANCE

WE CAN make our plans, but the Lord determines our steps.

PROVERBS 16:9 NLT

EVERY MOMENT you have a choice, regardless of what has happened before. Choose right now to move forward, positively and confidently into your incredible future. *Sometimes* you have to stop thinking and planning every little step, and just go in the direction your heart takes you because regardless of how every detail of the wedding works out, the one amazing thing remains. Once it's over, you'll be united with the love of your life and the dance of joy will be able to continue according to your hopes and dreams. Happy beginnings await!

The Wonder of Wedding Plans

We're making wedding plans
And everything is great,
We've found perfect invitations
And we've set the wedding date.

We've figured out the guest list,
And the grand reception hall,
And we'll have vases full of flowers
With vibrant colors of the fall.

We're excited with each step we take,
And filled with joy and hope,
But somehow all this planning,
Makes us want to just elope!

MAY YOUR wedding day and marriage
far exceed your plans.

ELIZABETH BARRETT BROWNING wrote
a wonderful poem to her husband,
Robert Browning, that has stood the test
of time to remind us of the joy of counting
the ways of understanding our love
for our partners.

How Do I Love Thee?
Let Me Count the Ways

How do I love thee? Let me count the ways.
I love thee to the depth and breadth and height
My soul can reach, when feeling out of sight
For the ends of Being and ideal Grace.
I love thee to the level of every day's
Most quiet need; by sun and candle-light.
I love thee freely, as men strive for Right;
I love thee purely, as they turn from Praise.
I love thee with the passion put to use
In my old griefs, and with my childhood's faith.
I love thee with a love I seemed to lose
With my lost saints,—I love thee with the breath,
Smiles, tears, of all my life!—and, if God choose,
I shall but love thee better after death.

AT THE TOUCH of love everyone becomes a poet.

PLATO

NO DOUBT YOU DID SOME DREAMING over the years about what your wedding day would be like. You may have changed your mind many times since then, but it's certain your hope would be to celebrate your love and your new life in the best possible ways. The good part is that you get to be in control, creating the perfect day for you.

Since planning and creating that day takes a lot of work, you may want to remember the unique and varied moments by going through a listing like the one that follows and noting a few memorable moments as you complete each step along the way. This isn't an exhaustive listing, but look at these as potential memory joggers for the things you are doing to make your big day glorious. Here are a few thing to think about as you put your plans together.

My Wedding Planning List

Setting the date, time, and place

Creating a budget and who will pay for which parts of your event

Creating a wedding website with updates and information pertinent to those who are part of the planning

Pre-marital counseling

Getting the marriage license

Finding the right person to officiate

Finding the best place for a reception

Setting the mood or theme or tone for the wedding, from country casual to city chic

Finding the perfect dress

Choosing the bridal party

Finding the right words for invitations and vows

Flowers and bridal bouquets

Menu planning

Setting up a gift registry

Celebrations and Showers

Favorite songs and musicians

Photographers and videographers

Honeymoon plans

YOU MAY HAVE many more things to put on your list. You'll discover that each step creates a new memory that builds a strong foundation for getting your marriage off to a great start.

Now, the next step is about finding the right words for your wedding invitation. Here are a few ideas you might consider and some words that might work best for you. The words in your wedding invitation can reflect the mood you set for the ceremony --- that mirrors your personalities in some way. If you happen to share a life work, like being in publishing or running a bookstore, or you're simply avid readers, you might design an invitation that looks something like a book cover and declares, "We're Starting a New Chapter."

If you both love camping or hiking or doing any number of things outdoors, you might go with a design that depicts a new path or a trail and then declares "Finding a New Path Together." Talk with your partner about the ways you experience life together and the things that make you unique as a couple. Your invitation can then be a personal keepsake for you and all who receive it.

Here are some lead phrases that may help you create a wedding invitation that reflects your love in a special way:

We Were Made for Each Other

We both said, "Yes!"

At Last, Love Has Come Along

From Now Until Forever

Planning a Lifetime of Love

From this Day Forward

Two Are Better Than One

Our Day Has Come

Happily Ever After

Love Has Found Us

Marrying My Best Friend

We're Ready to Say, "I Do"

Please Share Our Joy

We're Tying the Knot

It's Love for a Lifetime

Celebrate Our Love with Us

No More Lonely Nights

God Joined Us Together

We're Joined Heart to Heart

We Invite You to Celebrate Love with Us

THE BEAUTY of
your invitation,
or perhaps
your wedding
announcement
if you elope,
is that you draw
your friends
and family into
your celebration.
You can embrace
the future with
all the people that
mean the world
to you. Give yourself
time to create
something that
reflects the two
of you in a
unique way.

Place Your Invitation Here

YOU'VE MANAGED to do a lot of important planning that will make your special day memorable and exciting. You've created the mood and the atmosphere. You've got a sense of all the details needed to pull off the most significant event of your life. You've had fun creating some unique and special moments for those who will share your wedding festivities.

Chances are that those who received your invitation are celebrating with you and want to do something special for you as well. They may give you more than one wedding shower. These days, it's not uncommon to have everything from general household showers, lingerie showers, kitchen showers, and groom's showers. Everyone wants to be part of the fun. If that happens, be sure to bring a guest book with you to record who was there and any gifts you received. Here's a little listing of special showers someone may want to give for you.

The "something blue" shower, where every gift is a shade of blue

The "something old" shower, where everything is nostalgic

A chocolate buffet shower

The every bride needs a "toolbox" shower

The groom's handyman shower

Specialty themed showers for teachers, writers, artists, musicians, and others

A coupon-for-you shower where the bride is given unique coupons for things like manicures, haircuts, and floral arrangements, and house-sitting.

A kitchen shower

A fragrance shower

A linen shower

THERE ARE A VARIETY of ways to celebrate your upcoming marriage. Try to do anything that can make waiting for that big day special. Part of the beauty of being a bride is to celebrate in every way that will bring you laughter and joy.

Promises
and Vows

WHAT LOVING WORDS will you say as you become a lifetime Couple? You may not have ever imagined the words you and your lover would speak as you share your love at the altar. You probably hoped you could just be calm enough to get through it without fainting or stumbling over your vows. Perhaps you thought that the person officiating would take care of the specific words you would need to say.

But many couples prefer to create their own vows. If you want to get an idea of what couples have been saying to each other, here are a few examples:

I, (GROOM),
take you, (Bride),
to be my lifetime partner and wife.

I will share my life with yours,
look for ways to build our dreams together
and support you through times of difficulty.

I will always rejoice with you
in times of happiness.

I promise to give you my utmost respect, love and loyalty through all the trials and triumphs of our lives together.

I make this commitment to you with love, promise to keep it in faith, live it in hope, and make it anew every day of our lives.

I CHOOSE YOU _____ because of who you are and what you mean to me.

I commit to loving what I know of you, and trusting what I do not yet know.

I promise to respect you as an individual, a partner, and as my beloved, even more than my equal.

I promise to laugh with you when times are good, and hold on to you when they are difficult for us.

I commit to you that I will always adore you, honor you and encourage you in every way that I can.

You are my best friend, and I promise from this day forward to love you always.

Here's an example of sharing your vows in a responsive way.

GROOM: I promise to seek your advice and ask your help when I'm uncertain.

BRIDE: I promise to listen with love and share my own concerns.

GROOM: I promise to tell you what's on my mind so you don't have to guess.

BRIDE: I promise to give you time to sort out your feelings.

GROOM: I promise to surprise you now and then with flowers, or an unexpected date just to have fun.

BRIDE: I promise to always try to keep the sweet romance in our marriage.

GROOM: I promise to keep you number one in my life, above my job, and my favorite sports team.

BRIDE: I promise to make it easy to be your number one in any way I can, and to root for your favorite team sometimes.

GROOM: I promise to support you in whatever you choose to do.

BRIDE: I promise to support you in whatever you choose to do as well.

GROOM: I promise to pay attention to details, the little things that mean a lot to you.

BRIDE: I promise to try to see the big picture and embrace your vision for us.

GROOM: I promise to respect your mind and encourage your love of learning.

BRIDE: I promise to remind you of your talents and cheer for your successes.

GROOM: I promise to pray for you each day.

BRIDE: I promise to pray for you as well.

GROOM: I promise to tell you I love you and need you each day.

BRIDE: I promise to show you I care and that you matter always.

GROOM: I promise to seek your opinions and trust your judgment.

BRIDE: I promise to ask your advice and consider your suggestions.

GROOM: I promise to honor you, cherish you, and hold you in my heart forever.

BRIDE: I promise to hug you, kiss you, and cherish you always.

GROOM: I promise to love you from this day forward.

BRIDE: I promise to love you now and always.

BRIDE TO GROOM:
I promise you one hundred percent fidelity.

I will not covet what is not under our roof; you and our children will be enough.

I promise to give you soft kisses and warm hugs when times are tough, and lots of them each day just because I can.

I promise to never have a mid-life crisis and think that I have missed out; for I know I have not.

I promise I will be a good wife and share responsibility in all that we do.

I promise to be there for you and for our future children and grandchildren.

Lastly, I promise to admit when I am wrong and be a loving partner, always willing to compromise, so we can work together to solve our dilemmas and enjoy our successes.

GROOM TO BRIDE:
The life and love we've shared over the time of our courtship has made me feel so happy and content. Only having you as my wife would make me happier, and more complete.

I promise to make you laugh when you are sad, and to share your joy when you are happy. I promise to adore you, and cherish you, and to stand beside you through whatever our life together brings.

I take you to be my wife, knowing that my love for you will never falter, and only grow stronger with each day we share.

I promise I will be your faithful husband, always and forever, because nothing and no one will ever mean more to me than you do.

BRIDE TO GROOM:

Today I promise that our friendship and mutual devotion will be a foundation of our love through bad times and good times, and that nothing will be as important to me as living life with you.

Because of you, I finally understand what love is. It is the patience you show when I'm being stubborn and won't admit you're right, and it is the kindness in your eyes every time you look at me.

I love the complete trust you have in me and the respect you always show me wherever we are. Love is the hope and the belief that our futures are forever connected, and that you will be with me always.

Today, in front of all these people, I take you to be my friend and my husband, to love, to respect, to trust, to cherish and to hold above all others.

If (for the Bride and Groom)

If you can pledge to do your best
    To help each other through
The challenges that marriage brings
    That test the "I love you." ...

If you can give each other
    The freedom to keep growing,
And talk about the things you need
    To help you each keep going ...

If you can face the little things
    That come up, day by day,
And find you have the strength of two
    To chase them all away.

If you can look back where you've been
    And then look on ahead
And know that nothing matters more
    Than the joy of being wed...

Then you can have a marriage
    That's a blessing and a blend
Of love and joy and laughter,
    Heart to heart, and friend to friend.

YOU MAY ASK the person who officiates at your ceremony to offer a few words of wisdom for you to contemplate from that day forward. You may request stories to be shared by family and friends to make your ceremony more special to you both.

You may wish to recite vows as they are dictated to you, or you can speak words of love to each other, offered from the heart, meant to reflect all that you hope your life together will bring. Writing your own vows may seem challenging, but it can also be your gift to your new life together. It can embrace the heart of the moment and give voice to your own personal truths. Here are a few leads to contemplate if you write your vows:

I want you beside me always, no matter where life takes me.

My heart is only truly at home in you.

Home is wherever you are.

I will honor you with my heart and mind and body for always.

I will embrace all that you are and love you unconditionally.

With you, I have a new beginning, a new opportunity to be a kind and loving person every day.

I will say I'm sorry when I make a mess of things.

You are my heart, my joy, and the gift of love I always dreamed would be mine.

Years from now, I promise to love you even more than I do today.

I promise to hold you close to my heart forever. Only God could have designed a love like the one we share.

I vow to always speak kindness and love into your day, to help you move beyond any shadows that may appear.

You are the light that will shine in my heart from this day forward.

As we begin this adventure together, I promise to pack only love and hope and a spirit of joy to take with us wherever we go.

Of course, there are endless ways to say how you love each other. No matter what you say, the promises will live on in your hearts. You will pledge to honor, to sacrifice, to love and to do all you can to build a future of lasting happiness. A vow is a sacred pledge intended to stand firm no matter what life brings. Say your vows with infinite love, enormous grace for each other, and with the kind of hope that ushers in a radiant future.

I Promise You

A promise is a pledge,
A sacred, lasting vow,
And so I promise you my love,
And my commitment now.
I promise that I'll hold you
When any doubts appear,
And I promise that I'll be there
In moments that bring fear.
I promise that I'll see you,
As the person that you are,
And encourage all your dreams
So that they can take you far.

I promise to apologize
When I do something wrong
And I promise that I'll do my best
To keep you safe and strong.
I promise to embrace our lives
To bring you joy and laughter,
Because I promise from this day
To love you forever after!

THE BEAUTY OF PROMISES is that
you make them from the heart.
When things are uncertain, or
your relationship feels disconnected,
you can go back to those promises,
get grounded, and start again.
They will hold you up and remind you
of the places you meant to go.
They will help to sustain you
along the journey.

Our
Wedding
Day

BRIDE_____
AND
GROOM_____

WERE HAPPILY MARRIED

ON (DATE)_____

AT (PLACE)_____

IN (LOCATION)_____

OFFICIANT_____

ATTENDANTS_____

_____

_____

_____

_____

_____

MUSIC_____

_____

_____

FLOWERS_____

_____

Moments to Remember

Bride's Vows

Groom's Vows

SO, YOU MADE IT through the wedding without fainting or stumbling and the vows were beautiful and a few happy tears were shed. Indelible images have been printed on your heart that will remain with you forever and a day.

When the ceremony was over, you may have planned a reception in a fancy, beautifully decorated hall, or at a lovely restaurant, or perhaps in your home or at the church. You probably spent a little time sharing joy with your guests, talking with each one and celebrating this amazing moment in your life.

If you have a formal reception, or if you plan a small gathering after the wedding, you may have someone offer a toast. Sometimes it's the best man, sometimes it's your dad or even the maid of honor. They will share with tenderness and perhaps a little humor, what this day means to them and offer to honor you with a toast for your future.

If anyone asks for help with what to say as they create a toast, here are a few ideas that others have shared on this occasion. Perhaps this will help those who will choose to honor you on your wedding day.

A Toast for Joy

Share what your relationship is with the bride
and groom and share it from the heart.
Make it more about them than about you.

Describe some of the things that you believe
make them a truly great couple, things that they
will remember for always.

Don't say anything that might seem at all
embarrassing.

Remember to acknowledge their families,
especially their parents.

Offer the couple some tidbits of wisdom or
perhaps a favorite literary or Scripture quote.
Tug on their heartstrings and make them feel
good about the future.

Keep your toast under three minutes.

With great love and respect lift your glass
to the happy couple.

ONE WORD frees us of all the weight
and pain of life: That word is love.

SOPHOCLES

TO KEEP your marriage brimming,
with love in the wedding cup,
whenever you're wrong, admit it;
whenever you're right, shut up.

OGDEN NASH

AND NOW here is my secret, a very simple secret;
it is only with the heart that one can see rightly,
what is essential is invisible to the eye.

ANTOINE DE SAINT-EXUPERY

MARRIAGE is the golden ring in a chain
whose beginning is a glance and whose ending
is Eternity.

KAHLIL GIBRAN

SUCCESS in marriage does not come
merely through finding the right mate,
but through being the right mate.

BARNETT BRICKNER

THERE IS no more lovely, friendly, and
charming relationship, communion, or company
than a good marriage.

MARTIN LUTHER

A SUCCESSFUL marriage requires falling in love
many times, always with the same person.

MIGNON MCLAUGHLIN

LOVE ONE ANOTHER, but make not a bond of love:
Let it rather be a moving sea between the shores
of your souls

THE KNOT

HERE'S TO the new husband,
and here's to the new wife,
may they remain lovers,
for all of life.

MAY ALL YOUR hopes and dreams come true,
and may the memory of this day
become dearer with each passing year.

May the best of your yesterdays
be the worst of your tomorrows.

May the light of friendship guide your paths
together.

May the laughter of children grace the halls of
your home.

May the joy of living for one another trip a smile
from your lips, and a twinkle from your eye.

You've chosen to love for a lifetime, chosen to
learn and grow together, and chosen to keep
each other a priority. May all that you've chosen
be just the beginning of the joy you're meant to
share.

When the Wedding Day Is Over

Oh, the wedding day is over,
The vows have all been said,
The songs have filled the chapel
And the Scriptures have been read.

You're ready now to start again,
But this time not alone,
You're committed to each other
With a place to call your own.

You've stood before the altar
And promised all through life
To be each other's number one,
As a husband and a wife.

With rings upon your fingers
And smiles on your faces,
You're ready to embrace the world
In all your favorite places.

May you long remember all the gifts
Of your wedding day,
And may these forever fill your heart
With love to guide your way.

The Poem of Ben Jonson to Celia

Drink to me only with thine eyes
And I will pledge with mine;
Or leave a kiss but in the cup
And I'll not look for wine.
The thirst that from the soul doth rise
Doth ask a drink divine;
But might I of Jove's nectar sup,
I would not change for thine.

EVEN MIRACLES take a little time, so enjoy your beautiful beginning together. True love means you stand beside each other during the good times, and that you stand even closer to each other during the bad times because the most important part of the marriage comes after the ceremony, when life will give you chances to fall in love over and over again. Marriage means you have time to create happiness in any ways that you both choose, taking long walks, having long talks, and enjoying moments simply to recognize the gifts you have in each other. Now you have the opportunity to embrace life as you've never done before. What joy that brings!

Your New Life as
Husband and Wife

Building Bridges

Let us build with art and soul, my dear,
A bridge of faith between your life and mine,
A bridge of tender love and very near
A bridge of understanding strong and fine—
Till we have formed so many gentle ties
There never will be room for walls to rise.

THE IDEA OF A HONEYMOON actually dates back to a Scripture from Deuteronomy 24:5. "When a man is newlywed, he need not go out on a military expedition, nor shall any public duty be imposed on him. He shall be exempt for one year for the sake of his family, to bring joy to the wife he has married." It was believed that the new couple needed time alone without hindrance to become an established couple and to create a family.

The term 'honeymoon' as we know it, goes back to the 5th century AD and a time when the calendar was based on the cycles of the moon. A newly-married couple would be given plenty of mead to drink during their first month of married life. Mead is a mixture of one part honey and three parts water that fermented and became an alcoholic drink. It was believed if couples faithfully drank the mead that they would quickly bear healthy children, since mead was also known for its aphrodisiac properties.

In the 16th century, Samuel Johnson referred to the honeymoon period as, "...the first month after marriage, when there is nothing but tenderness and pleasure."

The contemporary practice of newlyweds taking a vacation together dates back to the days of the Raj in the Indian subcontinent. In the early 1800s, British imperialists based in India noticed an Indian class custom for newly married couples to take a "bridal tour." The couple would often be accompanied by others; the idea was to visit those friends and relatives who weren't able to attend the wedding.

Today, the honeymoon, whether it be a weekend, a week, or a longer vacation time, is considered to be an important time for the couple to leave friends and family behind, and to create bonds together that will carry them through life. That means it is very important for the couple to make their destination a place that will be well-suited to them both.

Honeymoon Ideas

An exotic beach

A mountain chateau

A cruise

A beautiful bed and breakfast

A bicycle trip

A spa

A cabin in the woods

Paris

Explore New England

Explore an historic U.S. city

Visit a world landmark

MOST IMPORTANT is for you to be alone—
together. The rest of your life begins with your
honeymoon.

The Honeymoon

The honeymoon was neatly planned,
Each detail strictly noted,
Everything was perfect,
At least as it was quoted.

Yet, no one said that it might rain,
Or flights would cause delay,
Or there'd be no reservation
At the place you hoped to stay.

But, nothing really mattered then,
Because everything was right,
For you were there sharing love
Morning, noon, and night.

Yes, plans can sometimes go awry
Or they may go perfectly,
But your honeymoon begins the life
Where all your dreams will be.

IT'S GOOD TO UNPACK your baggage, a little at a time. Being a first love is good, but being the last love is the best and now that you're off on your honeymoon you can begin the practice of giving and receiving patient and loving attention. After all, this is the gift that newlyweds bring to each other. Unpack great moments of joy wherever you go from here.

What Does Marriage Really Mean?

Marriage means that you create
The things that make love thrive,
You hold hands everywhere you go
And keep your love alive.

You work hard on the courtship
That never has to end
And walk beside each other,
Arm in arm, and friend to friend.

Marriage means you value
Each other's mind and heart
And that you feel a loss
Any time that you're apart.

It means you have a circle
Of new friends and family
That you both honor and regard
With love and loyalty.

Marriage means you understand
That when you know you're wrong,
You willingly apologize
So your love keeps growing strong.

Yes, marriage means you'll laugh a lot
And cry a little too,
But most of all and best of all,
You'll be glad you said, "I do!"

WELCOME TO YOUR FIRST HOME as Mr. and
Mrs. Whether you were sharing a living space
before the wedding, or whether you set up
housekeeping after the honeymoon, your
first home as a couple will always bring warm
memories and maybe a few conflicting ways
of living that you have to sort through. This will be
the home that sets the mood and the ambience
of the way you each share your relationship.
Perhaps you set up a few rules of who will
manage which aspects of the household duties,
who will pay the bills and how you will share the

housekeeping; who will do the cooking and who will do the yard work. The tasks you will share and the tasks you will do alone. This is the home where your story begins, the one you'll talk about for years to come.

Perhaps you will ask yourselves some questions like these:

How much space do we need?

How far are we willing to commute to work?

What style do we like in apartments or condos or houses?

What's your favorite color?

How important is it to have an office at home?

What kind of yard do we need?

Do we want our home in the country or the city?

Do we need to be close to an airport?

Do we want lots of neighbors?

Do we want to have pets?

Do we want a garden?

How can our home become our sanctuary, our love nest, away from the world?
Or a part of the world?

YOUR FIRST HOME is more than a place to hang your hat. It's the place where you will replenish your heart every day, the place where your day will begin and end on a loving note. It's your home and your style that's going to make your beginning beautiful. Make a promise to each other that your "home" will always be a joyful and sacred place to share.

EVERY HOUSE where love abides
And friendship is a guest,
Is surely home, and home sweet home
For there the heart can rest.

HENRY VAN DYKE

IT TAKES HANDS to build a house, but only hearts can build a home.

AUTHOR UNKNOWN

WHERE WE LOVE is home, home that our feet may leave, but not our hearts.

OLIVER WENDELL HOLMES

So Glad I'm Home!

Perhaps the sweetest words you'll say,
When you've been working hard all day
And found yourself forced yet to roam,
Are those sweet words, "So glad I'm home!"

Your home will always be your castle if you treat
each other like royalty.

Home Is the Place
Where Love Resides

Home is the place where love resides
In each floorboard, wall and rafter,
Home is the place you hang your heart
And fill your days with laughter.

Home is the place where hope stops by
In the smiles of family and friends,
Yes, home is the place where love resides
And joy just never ends.

Home Is Our Safe Haven

Home is where we sweep away
All the worries of the day

And with kind words and sweet delight
We guard each other through the night.

LEARNING TO LIVE IN HARMONY. The first few weeks after the wedding, may find each of you scrambling to get back into a sense of routine for your work life and for your life together. It may not be easy to get things running smoothly, especially if you've just moved into a new apartment or you've each been used to doing things in a certain way, a way you weren't quite prepared to change. You might need to manage your expectations of each other in ways you've never had to do before. Maybe one of you is meticulous about your living space, and the other one is much more casual. One of you likes to know that dinner is always at six, and the other likes spontaneous ideas about how and when to create the dinner hour. One of you is a gourmet cook and one of you has lived on take-out. You have a new life now, and this is where you discover what it means to live and work in harmony, allowing two people to become one family unit.

Setting Up Housekeeping

It's fun to pick new furnishings,
Or make hand-me-downs look cute,
But how we re-arrange our things
May cause a slight dispute.

I like to have things orderly,
Clean and neat and put away,
You like to be more casual,
A little mess is quite okay.

Now we have to work it out,
Create a home to share our bliss,
So let's give each other lots of space
And seal it with a kiss.

TO GET YOUR MARRIAGE OFF TO A GREAT START.
In the dating phase of your relationship, you probably were pretty protective of each other and of the feelings of connection you had established. You were intentional about what you did to please each other. You remembered special things that made a difference. You had little surprises to make each other feel good. You were conscious of paying attention to the details that helped you enjoy being together.

So what about now? Now that you're married, how can you keep that warm glow you felt during the courtship? How can you remain sweetly conscious of each other's needs? Here are some ideas for simple things you can do that may prove helpful the first year and all the years that follow.

Kiss

Don't forget to kiss each other...a lot! You may think that's a pretty easy thing to do, and of course, it should feel easy since you just got married. As time goes on though, it's something you never want to take for granted. You don't want to get so distracted by life circumstances that you forget how embraceable you are. Kiss each other hello in the morning and when you come home from work. Kiss each other any time you have to say goodbye for a while. Kiss each other just because you want to communicate a moment of happiness that you feel. Kiss each other with joy, with passion, with compassion and with an aim to remind each other of the great love you share.

Hug and Hold Hands

Sure, it sounds silly to imagine hugging all through the day, but sometimes spouses forget how important a hug can be to keep each other feeling content and connected in the marriage. Hug your partner spontaneously, lovingly, simply, sweetly, and often. Never let your spouse wonder if you are interested in keeping the closeness you shared when you dated. Hug and then hug a little bit more. It will always make things better.

When you walk somewhere, anywhere, hold hands. Hold hands to simply, wordlessly, joyfully share your hearts and your desire to be together. Hold hands when you have to discuss something that is important or difficult. Hold hands when you feel nervous or fearful about anything. Hold hands when you pray and hold hands when you shop at the mall. Hold each other close every day.

Say, "I love you."

Keep saying, "I love you." It's easier than you think to assume that once you're married, you must obviously love each other so you don't have to say it. The truth is you both need to hear those words spoken frequently. You need to remind each other that the love you share is the most essential part of your day, the thing that keeps you thriving and growing stronger. Say the "L" word every chance you get and your marriage will last a lifetime.

Surprise each other

Yes, those little things mattered when you were dating and they may matter even more now. Now you have the person of your dreams in your life, sharing your daily routine. What can you do to add surprise and delight to any day? Leave a love note under a pillow, tucked in a shirt pocket or hanging on the fridge. Buy the coconut, chocolate delights from your favorite candy store or the coffee ice cream you don't even like. These are the things that will put a smile on your loved one's face.

Keep a Journal

As often as possible, sit down together and talk over the events of the day or the week, or even the month. Write down in a shared journal what the event was and how you each felt about it. Put a star next to the ones that were really special so that when you're having a difficult day sometime in the future, you can go back and remind yourselves of that day, and maybe re-capture that moment again. Over time, you'll have the story of how your love has grown and how it established the foundation you have created as a couple.

FAITH makes all things possible...
love makes all things easy.

DWIGHT L. MOODY

When I Need Your Love

I need your loving in the morning
Before my day begins,
Just holding me close
Starting with grins... it brings such perfect joy.

I need your loving in the noontime
When the world gets in the way,
When things feel more uncertain
And I struggle with the day...
    because you make all the difference.

I need your loving in the evening
When the day is through
Because nothing in the world makes sense

Till I'm wrapped up in you…
    because you are my love!
Thanks for loving me… always.

YOU MAY THINK that "living happily ever after" is the stuff of fairy tales, but it can be your tale if you choose to create your life with love every day. Love will sustain you and love will lead you on into the future. And before you know it, you'll be celebrating your First Year.

Your first anniversary is a sweet milestone and you will want to celebrate it with joy, building on the memories you've already gathered as a couple. As you celebrate your happy beginning and go into the next year of your marriage, here are a few ideas to keep you going on that road to "happily ever after."

Ideas for Date Nights

Pull out a calendar and pick one night each month for a special date night. Take turns planning something romantic and fun.

Coupons—create your own book of twelve coupons for special times that you have shared over the year. Create coupons that reflect the special events you enjoyed over the first year of your marriage. Repeat those activities in your next year by "cashing in your coupon!"

Brainstorm with each other about the things you like to do together that make you laugh, or help you feel romantic and connected, or simply are of mutual interest. Color code the ideas by the type they are, even coding them further for which ones you can do for under $10.00 and which ones are over $50.00. Write your ideas on separate papers and keep them in a jar to draw them out when you want something special to do.

Create your own story book of the things you did that were special to each of you and to the two of you during your first year. It could help you write a Christmas letter, but save it so you can enjoy those memories for many years to come.

Other Ways to Celebrate Your Anniversaries

Plan a special event for later in the coming year to give you both something to look forward to. Make a collage of some of your wedding pictures and frame them for your home.

Get a chalkboard and make a list of rules for your house. For example, "In this house, we always kiss goodnight, good morning, and good afternoon!"

Invite the people who participated in your wedding to share their memories of your wedding day.

Take a photo of the two of you each year so you can see how you've changed and grown through the years.

Set aside a special time for the two of you to look back over the year and talk about the things you did that you don't want to do again and those things you'd like to do more of. Plan to do more of the good things.

Eat that wedding cake you put in the freezer.

Repeat your vows to each other. Do this every year and affirm your marriage often.

It's a good time to pop open some bubbly champagne, perhaps followed by a bubbly bath.

When you do things that keep your marriage vibrant and strong, you protect it from the challenges of life, and create bonds of closeness that can never be broken.

Thoughts to share as you reminisce about your marriage

You may not be perfect, but you're perfect for me.

The best choice I ever made was the choice to love you forever.

I keep falling in love with you...
and I'm so grateful!

I loved you on our wedding day
And I love you even more today.

Marriage may require work,
but it's a job that has amazing benefits.

You're the best part of my life and you always will be.

I would marry you again in a heartbeat.

My heart will always be at home with you.

BEING DEEPLY LOVED by someone gives you strength, while loving someone deeply gives you courage.

LAO TZU

THE MOST WONDERFUL of all things in life, I believe, is the discovery of another human being with whom one's relationship has a glowing depth, beauty and joy as the years increase. This inner progressiveness of love between two human beings is a most marvelous thing, it cannot be found by looking for it. It is a sort of Divine accident.

SIR HUGH WALPOLE

NOTHING IS SWEETER than Love, nothing stronger, nothing higher, nothing wider, nothing more pleasant, nothing fuller nor better in heaven and earth.

THOMAS A' KEMPIS

ONE WORD frees us of all the weight and pain in life. That word is love.

SOPHOCLES

THIS IS THE MIRACLE that happens every time to those who really love; the more they give, the more they possess.

RAINER MARIA RILKE

Your First Anniversary

The first anniversary
 Is a precious milestone;
A measure of the things you've shared
And all the ways you've grown.

It's the perfect chance to reminisce,
Tell stories of the wedding,
And share again a special kiss
In joy at where you're heading.

Your first anniversary
Celebrates you two,
As a reminder of the life and love
That's still ahead of you.

YOUR MARRIAGE is meant to move from joy to joy. If you can imagine a life where each of you honors the other, where you put each other first, and you seek each other's counsel when things aren't quite what you hope they can be, then it's possible to live each day in real joy. It's possible because you'll be choosing to live in harmony and to make more room in your hearts each day for each other.

Certainly, you'll experience life with setbacks and unexpected disappointments, but you don't have to stay there. Part of being two is that you have each other to help no matter what circumstances arise. There's a wonderful Scripture that comes from Ecclesiastes four and it says this:

TWO PEOPLE CAN ACCOMPLISH more than twice as much as one; they get a better return for their labor. If one person falls, the other can reach out and help. But people who are alone when they fall are in real trouble. And on a cold night, two under the same blanket can gain warmth from each other. But how can one be warm alone? A person standing alone can be attacked and defeated, but two can stand back-to-back and conquer.

ECCLESIASTES 4:9-12 NLT

FROM NOW ON, you have a companion, a helper, someone who is paying attention to you, who knows you well and seeks your good. Love does not dominate; it cultivates.

GOETHE

LOVE IS a condition in which the happiness of another person is essential to your own.

ROBERT HEINLEIN

LOVE NEVER CLAIMS, it ever gives; love never suffers, never resents, never revenges itself. Where there is love there is life.

MAHATMA GANDHI

You will find, as you look back upon your life, that the moments when you really lived are the moments when you have done things in the spirit of love.

HENRY DRUMMOND

Real love is a force more formidable than any other. It is invisible—it cannot be seen or measured, yet it is powerful enough to transform you in a moment, and offer you more joy than any material possession could.

BARBARA DEANGELIS

YOU MAY HAVE DREAMED of a perfect love. It would be the kind of love that would always meet *your* expectations, embrace *your* ideals, and never disappoint *you*. Perfect love would simply grow and move in the right direction to become everything *you* always wanted.

Then one day, you came to understand that perfect love doesn't actually exist, probably not even in fairy tales. Now you have experienced enough of life to realize that love doesn't have to be perfect at all. Your loved one doesn't have to be superhuman to meet your needs. You *share* a love that becomes the most that REAL love can be.

Real love is a seeker. Real love embraces imperfections, challenges truth, forgives slights and sees the beauty of your very soul.

Real love digs deeper to discover even more ways to share its gifts, seeking every possibility and every chance for tenderness. Real love is a heart laid bare, exposed, with a will to be made... perfect...in the arms of love. May your love for each other, become the real love that sustains your marriage for now and forever. You never need accept imitations.

LOVE ISN'T A STATE of perfect caring. It is an active noun like struggle. To love someone is to strive to accept that person exactly the way he or she is, right here and now.

FRED ROGERS

LOVE IS LIFE. And if you miss love, you miss life.

LEO BUSCAGLIA

YOU KNOW IT'S LOVE when you want to keep holding hands, even after you're hands are sweaty.

AUTHOR UNKNOWN

THE BEST THING to hold on to in life
is each other.

AUDREY HEPBURN

FROM NOW ON, you are your husband's bride, his
life partner and companion. Your future will be
built one day at a time, one decision at a time,
and one smile at a time. How will you protect
what you have? How will you ensure that you
have a marriage that is sustainable, and one that
can last a lifetime? You have tools to use that
can help you at any time to create a strong and
loving marriage.

Express your feelings. Whether you have good
things to say or difficult things to say, you can
get lost in an effort to find the right words to
express how you feel. The right words may not
be the most important thing. After all, spoken
words are less than half of any real conversation.
Everything you need to communicate happens
in your heart and is shared by your face, by your
eyes, by your stance and by your hands. Your
body language speaks loudly and conveys the
meaning of what you want to say.

Tips to Keep Your Love Alive

Remember that your partner loves you and wants you to be happy. Start with the premise that you are in a safe place and talking with someone who totally accepts who you are and wants to know and love you better. Keep talking. Keep listening. Imagine that your heart has ears and is hearing everything, what's said and what isn't said at all. Compassionate communication sustains your relationship and strengthens you to face life's challenges together.

Remember that your marriage is the place to learn about love, and to teach each other what love really means. Don't be afraid to step out in faith to help each other keep the promises you've made together. You made those vows knowing that some days would be less exciting, less fulfilling than others. You're in it for the marathon, the distance, and not just the sprint.

Give each other room to make mistakes and to find new ways to grow together

Be intentional about your relationship, committing yourselves to it fully

Try to change one habit you know drives your partner crazy

Mail a romantic card to the office

Relive the moments of when you first met

Carry a love note from your spouse in your wallet at all times

Practice adoring each other, when you're together or apart

Be playful

Be observant and supportive

Plan a getaway

Talk about everything

Laugh a lot

Dance in the kitchen

Share your secrets

Say "I love you" in other languages

Step out of your comfort zone to express love

Share what you love about each other the most

Don't be afraid to be spontaneous

Give each other reasons to smile

WE LIVE IN A CULTURE where marriages are not given priority, and are often not sustainable. But, your marriage is different. You're going to make your marriage a success because the two of you are committed to each other's happiness. That commitment will carry you through every life experience. Give each other endless grace and love and the future will be yours.

AND NOW THESE THREE REMAIN: faith, hope, and love. But the greatest of these is love.

1 CORINTHIANS 13:13

WHEN WE are in love, we seem to ourselves quite different from what we were before.

BLAISE PASCAL

LOVE IS an act of endless forgiveness, a tender look which becomes a habit.

PETER USTINOV

WHERE THERE IS great love,
there are always miracles.

WILLA CATHER

THERE IS only one happiness in life—
to love and to be loved.

GEORGE SAND

EVERYTHING I understand, I understand only
because I love.

LEO TOLSTOY

The Tapestry of Marriage

Marriage is a tapestry
Woven with such care,
That everything is intertwined
With loving things you share.

Time is a weaver
And it threads each thing you do
With ribbons of remembrance
And pearls of wisdom too.

Before you know it happened,
You're a couple on your own,
With a history of lace-filled dreams
And special ways you've grown.

Each of you weave separate dreams
Sweetly into one
Creating precious memories
Of all the things you've done.

Yes, it started with your wedding day
When you each held a thread,
And started weaving stories
For all the days ahead.

SPREAD LOVE everywhere you go. First of all in your own house...let no one ever come to you without leaving better and happier. Be the living expression of God's kindness; kindness in your face, kindness in your eyes, kindness in your smile, kindness in your warm greeting.

MOTHER TERESA

LOVE BEGINS at home.

ANDRIA TERRENCE

LOVE IS the fulfillment of all works. There is the goal; that is why we run; we run toward it, and once we reach it, in it we shall find rest.

AUGUSTINE OF HIPPO

MAY YOU BOTH REMEMBER your wedding day as the beginning of joy, the moment when you made the best choice of your life. May you each be a loving gift, and an adoring presence, for each other for the rest of your lives.

Important Marriage Memories

Important Marriage Memories